R&R: The Ultimate Travel Guide for Military and Veterans

By David C. Moore

Copyright © 2015, 2016, 2017
by David C. Moore

Although the author and publisher have made every effort to ensure that the information in this book was correct at press time, the author and publisher do not assume and hereby disclaim any liability to any party for any loss, damage, or disruption caused by errors or omissions, whether such errors or omissions result from negligence, accident, or any other cause.

Visit
www.MilitaryTravelTips.com
for up to date military and travel discounts.

Table of Contents

Introduction 1

Tips for Flying Commercial Airlines 4

USO Lounges 5

Discounted Fares and Free Luggage on Commercial Airlines for U.S. Military 9

TSA Precheck 15

Best Military Auto Rental Discounts 17

Travel Free with Space-A Flying 24

Stay Cheap with Space-A Lodging 33

Free or Discounted Camping 41

Free Access to National Parks 49

Information, Tickets, and Tours 59

Morale, Welfare, and Recreation Programs 66

Favorite Travel Apps for Military and Retirees 71

Top West Coast Military Only Beaches 79

Disney: Big Discounts from Mickey 85

Hawaiian Holiday: Dream of an Oahu Vacation 91

Tokyo Travel: The New Sanno Hotel 98

Korean Getaway: The Dragon Hill Lodge 105

Alpine Adventure: Edelweiss Lodge and Resort 110

Packing for a Short Getaway: Military Style 116

Best Military Discounts and Resources 124

Introduction

This is an updated and expanded edition of this travel guide. After first publishing, the feedback was resounding request for even more information. The travel guide is now 50% longer and packed full of more tips and discounts.

The discounts and benefits available to military personnel and veterans are nearly endless. A simple Google search will overwhelm you with all the advertisements, websites, and discounts. This book is intended to parse through the outdated, conflicting, and numerous resources available and provide you with only the necessary information you need to plan your next vacation.

As an active or retired member of the United States military or family member of one, you are entitled to a lot of great discounts and benefits. From special travel deals to discounts on tickets and tours, you can enjoy these perks with the help of your military ID or veteran ID card.

These discounts are meant to thank members for their current or previous service to the nation. Some benefits come directly from the military or government as enticements for members to remain in the service. Long hours, deployments, and trainings away from family are common, so the military strives to ensure there are opportunities for service members to get away for some much-needed Rest and Recuperation.

In addition to government-provided discounts, many private and commercial organizations also offer discounts as ways to say "thank you" to the men and women in uniform. We'll touch on these as well in the book.

Tips for Flying Commercial Airlines

As a member of the military, you are probably used to travel. From navigating busy airports to passing the time on long international flights, you already have the routine down pat. If you have to travel by plane, there are some great discounts that can make the process a lot more budget-friendly. With benefits such as

USO lounges, waived or discounted baggage fees, and TSA Prechecks, commercial flights are about to get way easier thanks to your military service.

USO Lounges

When you travel do you get tired, hungry, and a bit cranky? Does it get harder and more difficult to be patient in crowded places? Don't worry! You are normal. Traveling and waiting in crowded places (such as airports) can be overwhelming for anyone.

The United Services Organization (USO) is a nonprofit group that works hard to make life a little better for military service members around the world. The USO has provided entertainment for troops by planning and sponsoring performances from artists, singers and comedians, and by planning other service-oriented projects.

One of their best initiatives is the addition of USO lounges in airports in 10 countries and 30 states. These lounges vary from simple private waiting rooms to upscale centers with sleeping areas, showers, and laundry facilities.

You can find USO lounges in many major airports across the United States. Some are located before security checkpoints while others are inside the terminal. They range from small and cozy to spacious and luxurious. Each USO lounge is staffed with volunteers that will help make your travels a little easier. They will set you up with drinks, snacks, Wi-Fi, and whatever else you need to make that long layover more bearable. Some of the lounges even have movie rooms or children's play areas, offering a nice break for the whole family. Military members and their families can enjoy these special private lounges around the world.

These lounges cut down on travel anxiety for a family by providing a sanctuary from the airport madness. Their donated food and snacks save you money on overpriced airport foods. Some lounges are even equipped with a kitchen to cook hot meals by the volunteers. I often enjoy a hot breakfast sandwich before an early flight at a USO lounge.

Going Overseas? USO lounges are international. International travel can be challenging with longer flights, delays, language barriers, unfamiliarity with currencies, and time zone changes. For this reason USO lounges located in the "most-traveled" zones for military personnel are ready and available for military members and their families. Visit the USO website to learn about USO lounge centers in Europe, the Pacific and in Southwest Asia. You might be surprised to find a USO lounge at an international location along your travels.

Don't forget to thank the volunteers there for all their dedication! Military members who know the value of true service may be inspired to realize that the USO lounges across the world employ a small amount of employees (around 400) and that many of the staff members on hand are volunteers. It's a fact for which to be thankful. On a trip to their next destination military members can enjoy the peace, security and comfort of a USO lounge and thank someone who, like them, is performing a valuable service.

For a list of all the airports with available USO lounges. Visit http://www.uso.org/Centers/USO-Centers---United-States.aspx

Discounted Fares and Free Luggage on Commercial Airlines for U.S. Military

If you've ever flown commercial airlines within the U.S. you know that traveling via air with luggage can add up when it comes to travel expenses. One of the valuable benefits of being a military member (or in some cases a Veteran) is receiving FREE luggage carrying services on commercial airlines. There are some airlines there may have exceptions and specific luggage sizes and weights but typically the free luggage option is straight forward. For all of the below information, it is always advised to check the airline's website for latest information.

Before You Leave for Work Travel or Vacation
As a part of your travel plans and preparations visit the www.GSA.gov site to learn more about the latest luggage carrying rules, regulations, standards and discounts. This article also outlines some of the general policies of popular commercial airlines available to U.S. citizens

and military personnel. It offers a quick overview of baggage allowance information.

Alaska Airlines

Alaska Airlines provides a fantastic deal for active-duty military personnel of up to five baggage items free. More specific information can be found via the Alaska Airlines website (www.alaskaair.com) and all benefits also apply to dependents of military personnel. This benefit also applies to military dependents with ID and travel orders.

American Airlines, American Eagle and American Connection

American Airlines offers a baggage allowance for military personnel, the first and second bags checked in with no additional charges. The general size and weight requirements standardized by American Airlines will still need to be observed. It's good practice to check current "checked baggage policy" before travel.

With American Airlines active-duty military dependents also obtain the same travel benefits. Before you plan travel with American Airlines call 800-433-7300 to check on their current luggage carrying policies.

Delta

In most cases, military personnel flying Delta receive four to five checked bags for free. Contact a Delta representative for more information. Before travelling with Delta contact 800-221-1212 regarding domestic travel or 800.241-4141 regarding international travel. www.delta.com

Frontier Airlines

Frontier Airlines provides reduced (military) fares to all card carrying Active Duty members and full reimbursements if travel plans change. To learn more about reduced rates contact the Frontier Airlines Reservation Call Center at 800-432-1359. There are no baggage frees for active-duty military. Regular size and weight restrictions on baggage must also be observed. www.flyfrontier.com

Jet Blue
When active-duty military personnel travel due to official travel then Jet Blue will waive baggage fees for up to 5 bags. If travelling for leisure this baggage allowance drops to 2 bags. The same restrictions apply to family members. Check with Jet Blue before travelling to learn about the latest fares. Call 1-800-JETBLUE and they will provide the latest information related to military personnel. If you are a member of Veteran's Advantage, then you will receive a 5% discount on fares as well. JetBlue also offers military fares. www.jetblue.com

Southwest Airlines
Southwest airlines is known for its economy flight packages and often chosen by those looking to travel for less. It already offers all

passengers two checked bags for free. For military is broadens this limit and military may check more than two pieces of luggage. In addition to more bags, Southwest offers military fares for all military personnel and their dependents. Military personnel must be on active duty to obtain these benefits and it is advised that travelers call 1-800-I-FLY-SWA (1-800-435-9792) to inquire about the latest military fares and size/weight restrictions on baggage. www.southwest.com

United Airlines

Active U.S. military personnel and their accompanying dependents, not traveling on official business, receive waived service charges for up to three checked bags at 70 pounds. This baggage allowance increases if you are flying United Economy or United First Class. Active U.S. military personnel dependents traveling are also exempt from fees as long as they are traveling on the same reservation. This exemption does not apply to group reservations with ten or more travelers. You can view more information at United's website (www.united.com). If you are a member of Veteran's Advantage, then you will receive a 5% discount on fares as well.

U.S. Airways

U.S. Airways offer discounted rates to active-duty military personnel and to military personnel on excused absence. The airline also provides discounted rates to discharged personnel as long as the discharge has taken place within a seven-day period. Dependents of military personnel also are eligible. It is best to check with the U.S. Airways website and baggage policy before travel but in general the first and second bags will be checked for FREE and if dependents are traveling by order then the first through the fourth bags are also checked for FREE. Visit the U.S. Airways website for more information. www.aa.com

TSA Precheck

One of the biggest hassles in any airport is navigating the Transportation Security Agency (TSA) checkpoints. The good news is the TSA has a Precheck program at many airports that will let you get through the process much faster. To enjoy this benefit, you must be an active duty service member and present your DoD ID number as a "known traveler number" when you make your travel reservations. Commercial airlines may not ask for this information, so make sure you volunteer it so that you will be registered for the TSA Precheck.

When you are eligible for the TSA Precheck program, you will get through security much faster. You won't have to remove your shoes, take out your laptop, or remove your jacket or belt. You don't have to be in uniform to quality for the expedited screening, and if you are on active duty and traveling with family members, children aged 12 and under can go through expedited screening too. For more information on TSA Precheck, visit www.tsa.gov/tsa-precheck/members-military.

Best Military Auto Rental Discounts

You may begin your travels with a flight, but an auto rental will give you the freedom to explore your destination. For members of the military and/or for veterans there are a variety of discounts available.

Hertz Military Auto Rental Discounts
Whether you're looking to rent a full size, economy, compact, standard or special vehicle there are discounts available at Hertz. These discounts are available for members of the U.S. military.

Military travelers can plan their next business or vacation destination and take advantage of the Hertz auto rental discounts by registering as a member of the Hertz website (www.hertz.com). When registering a military employee discount code number (CPD) will be requested so input "1910991" for Federal government. On subsequent visits to the website when military personnel book additional car rentals the CPD number will be "remembered" by the system so discounts can be obtained without any hassle.

Other Hertz benefits for military employees include space available upgrades and complimentary membership in the Hertz Gold Plus Rewards group.

Budget Auto Rental Discounts for Veterans
For veterans who are looking to get out of the house and travel the globe, Budget provides "the wheels" to get you there. Budget provides up to 25% off auto rentals for U.S. Veterans through Veterans Advantage. To plan a trip,

Veterans should enroll in Veterans Advantage program to save on rentals anywhere in the U.S. and in all participating International venues. Once Veterans are enrolled, Budget will provide even more savings with coupons that can be used in addition to regular discounts.

You will also want to sign up for the Budget Fastbreak service so you can skip the rental counter and head straight to the driver's wheel. Veterans can sign up for the Budget Fastbreak service by contacting a Budget representative and asking about the service. www.budget.com

For Veterans and Active-duty Military Personnel Enterprise Provides Military Auto Rental Discounts
Enterprise provides discounted rates on auto rentals for both active-duty military personnel AND Veterans. Enterprise provides year-round discounts for Veterans, Active Duty, National

Guard, the Reserve and their families; A great deal not to be missed!

Enterprise is also a partner in the Veterans Advantage program. Through the program, Veterans are also entitled to the following benefits:

-Free pick-up and delivery services from all Enterprise locations

-24-hour roadside assistance

-Discounted rates at over 7,000 Enterprise locations in five countries and (of course) all U.S. locations

-Service at 230 on-site airport locations throughout the nation and in Canada, the U.K., Germany and Ireland

-Wide variety of vehicles including 4x4s, minivans and luxury vehicles

-Monthly or long-term rental rates

To receive these Veterans-only benefits, Veterans should enroll in the Veterans

Advantage. Once enrolled, Veterans will be provided with an Enterprise Corporate Discount Number that will be utilized during the rental process for increased savings. Contact Enterprise regarding Veterans' discounts (or active-duty discounts) if you have any questions. www.enterprise.com

Alamo Provides Best Military Auto Rental Discounts

Like Hertz, Alamo offers auto rental discounts to various military groups. With Alamo, discounts can be obtained when traveling on official business or in conjunction with tour-of-duty orders. According to the Alamo website (www.alamo.com), for business travel you can expect the following Alamo benefits:

-No additional driver fees
-No underage driver fees
-Collision Damage Waiver (CDW) included
-Frequent Traveler benefits with Alamo's major

travel partners

-Over 550 participating locations worldwide to accommodate on-duty travel needs

To achieve these amazing deals active-duty military members must provide a government-issued ID or credit card. If these forms of ID are not provided then the official travel orders will be required. When shopping online for an auto rental, military personnel should use the phrase, Contract ID "GOVBIZ" to receive the best rate.

Alamo's discounted car rentals are also available to military personnel traveling on leisure:

-Discounted rates for federal government employees and military personnel.

-Frequent Traveler benefits with Alamo's major travel partners.

-Over 550 participating locations worldwide.

-Family members with dependent identification are also eligible for leisure rates.

A military ID will be required at the time of pick up. The minimum age for driving Alamo vehicles is standard (21 minimum age and drivers under the age of 25 may incur additional expenses). To make reservations with Alamo call 1-800 GO ALAMO or visit the Alamo website.

USAA and Military Auto Rental Discounts
In addition to Hertz and Alamo, USAA offers discounted car rentals to military personnel and its members. For the latest discounted rates for military personnel contact an USAA representative. USAA also provides military personnel with the following:

-Discounted credit card rates
-Discounted auto insurance www.usaa.com

Travel Free with Space-A Flying

As an active or retired member of the United States military, you have the option to travel on military flights for no charge when space is available. This Space-A travel opportunity is a great choice if you want to take a trip to Hawaii, Alaska, or even overseas to Japan or Germany. The key is that you must be flexible on your travel dates and be prepared to face delays or even cancellations. You can't reserve seats for a Space-A flight, but you can register for the flight and then be granted a seat if there is room after necessary personnel have already boarded.

Who Can Use Space-A Flying?

These flights are available to active and retired service members, Department of Defense employees, and even family members in some situations. If you are part of the National Guard or the Reserve, you may be eligible for Space-A flights, but there are restrictions.

Space-A flights travel from military terminals, so you will have to register for flights directly at the terminal from which you wish to fly. Each terminal has its own rules for the Space-A program, so it's important to contact the base ahead of time and ask for details. Military flight information is not publicly released online, so you will have to call the terminal to request information about your desired travel plans. For the best chances of getting a Space-A seat, opt for a busy terminal that regularly schedules flights on a daily basis.

In terms of cost, you can usually fly for free as a Space-A passenger, but there are exceptions. If you are flying to another country, you might have to pay a departure tax. You should also remember that inflight meals are usually not provided for Space-A travelers, so you might want to inquire about purchasing a boxed meal ahead of time.

You will need your military ID and a copy of your leave orders (if applicable). Family members will need a letter from the service member's commanding officer to verify their eligibility for Space-A travel. If you are an eligible Guard or Reserve member, you will need a copy of DD Form 1853. Lastly, make sure you bring your passport and travel visa if going overseas.

How to Book a Space-A Flight

The first step to travel as a Space-A passenger is to register at the military terminal. You can register as far as 60 days in advance of the flight date, and you should do so as soon as possible to get the best chance at being awarded a seat. When you go to register, you will need a valid military ID and paperwork to show your leave status (if applicable). Occasionally, terminals will allow you to register by e-mail or fax, but call to get specific requirements at the terminal from which you plan to fly.

Once you have registered for a Space-A seat, the terminal will assign you a passenger category. They use this system to determine the priority of assigned seats. Category 1 passengers get a higher priority than Category 2, 3, 4, and so on. Here is a quick overview of the categories and how they are determined.

Category 1 – The top priority for Space-A seats are given to active duty service members and their family members that are traveling because of an emergency leave.

Category 2 – These passengers are military personnel and accompanying family members that need to travel on Environmental Morale Leave. If circumstances force a service member or an immediate relative stationed internationally to return to the US, they get classified as Category 2.

Category 3 – This category is for service members and relatives that are on ordinary leave or a reenlistment leave. Family members of military personnel that have been deployed for a year or more (consecutively) are also in this category.

Category 4 – Family members that are traveling without service members due to EML orders are in this category. You will also be classified as Category 4 if you are a relative of a service member that has been deployed for more than 120 days.

Category 5 – These passengers are students with sponsors stationed in Hawaii or Alaska. This category also covers students that are actively enrolled in a trade school in the United States with a sponsor currently stationed overseas.

Category 6 – Last priority goes to retired military personnel and their family members. This would include Guard and Reserve members as well. This category is for flights within the United States, including Alaska, Hawaii, and other US territories.

What to Expect on a Space-A Flight

When your travel date arrives, arrive at the terminal several hours before the flight. Check in at the passenger counter to make sure your registration and documents are all in order. Then settle in and wait until the Space-A seats are determined. In some cases, the seats will be assigned up to three hours before the flight leaves, so you want to be there in time to get a spot if it's available.

Be prepared for a long day and bring along some distractions, especially if you are flying with small children. There could be long periods of waiting to find out if you get a seat on the flight. You might also have to wait for delayed flights. In some cases, military flights can be delayed for days; they may even have to make an unscheduled stop.

Furthermore, be flexible with your travel plans. There are no guarantees that you will get a seat on the flight, so you need to have a backup plan. Always bring along cash and credit cards in case you need to secure a hotel room or even a commercial flight to return home. You cannot stay overnight in passenger terminals, so be prepared to seek other accommodations during long flight delays. Keep in mind that your flight accommodations can vary drastically depending on the plane you are assigned. You might be on a comfortable, upscale passenger plane, but there's also a chance you might be traveling in the cargo hold of a C-130.

For the best chance of getting a seat, try to travel when military schools are in session. Avoid holidays or summer vacations as flights are generally full during these peak times of year.

Ultimately, Space-A flying can save you a lot of money, and it can be a major asset if you are forced to travel unexpectedly due to emergency leaves. Whether you are a retired service member or on active duty, Space-A flights can benefit you on your next travel adventure.

Web Resources

Air Mobility Command – www.amc.af.mil/amctravel/
Space-A Travel on Military Travel – www.militaryonesource.mil/mwr?content_id=268596

Stay Cheap with Space-A Lodging

As a member of the United States military, you can enjoy a relaxing getaway without spending a fortune thanks to Space-Available lodging options all over the world. This is one of the most incredible benefits for active and retired service members, but it often goes unnoticed. Most military installations have lodging facilities hosted by a branch—and no, not barracks. Hotels!

Most Space-A lodging can be booked online, but each lodging facility may have different time frames for posting vacancies.

Who Can Use Space-A Lodging?

This military benefit is available for all branches of military service. Whether you are a Reservist traveling for leisure, on leave from active duty, or a retired Navy veteran, you can plan your next vacation with the help of Space-A lodging at military-owned accommodations worldwide. With your military identification card, you can start planning the trip of a lifetime! Space-A lodging is generally open to the following individuals:

– Travelers on military orders
– Active and retired members of the Army, Air Force, Marines, Navy, Coast Guard, and Department of Defense
– National Guard and Army Reserve personnel
– Family members of active and retired military personnel
– Widows and widowers of military members

What Accommodations Does Space-A Lodging Offer?

You can find practically every kind of lodging imaginable through the Space-A program. From hotel rooms to campgrounds to recreational accommodations, there are facilities available across the United States and even in various countries around the world where you can stay for a drastically reduced price as a member of the US military. Here is a quick look at some of the most common accommodations offered on a Space-A basis.

Installation Lodging – If you are traveling on official business or your family is in the midst of moving because of new station orders, you can stay at military-installation facilities located on military bases around the country. When there is available room, they will offer accommodations for vacationers.

Recreational Lodging – These accommodations are designed specifically to offer military service members a serene vacation when you need it most. You will find destinations ranging from a lakefront cottage in the mountains to a beautiful beach cottage on the shores of Hawaii. Some facilities will even provide rental equipment such as surfboards or fishing tackle at a reduced rate. Specific recreational lodging resorts are discussed in later chapters.

Space-A Lodging for Your Branch of Service

Each branch of the military has its own unique approach to Space-A lodging. Here is a quick look at some of the options that you have and how you can start planning your trip.

Air Force Inns – Space-A lodging is available for active and retired military members in worldwide Air Force Inns. The accommodations are nice and clean and similar to what you would find in any basic hotel. To inquire about reservations, you can call 888-235-6343 or visit af.dodlodging.net.

Army Lodging – The Army offers 39 lodging locations, most of which are managed through the Intercontinental Hotels Group. They also have three CONUS accommodation programs at Ft. Lee, Ft. Benning, and Charlottesville. To make reservations, you can call 800-462-7691 or visit army.dodlodging.net.

Marine Corps Lodging – The Marine Corps provides short-term lodging accommodations for military personnel and their families. To find out about availability, visit innsofthecorps.com.

Navy Gateway Inns and Suites – Visit 74 locations around the world and stay in one of the 27,000 guest rooms offered through the Navy's Space-A lodging program. Reservations go quickly, and the rooms are approved on a first-come, first-serve basis. You can reserve a room up to a month in advance by calling 877-NAVY-BED or visiting ngis.dodlodging.net.

How to Reserve Your Space-A Lodging Accommodations

For the most part, each branch of the military has its own unique lodging program. To get the best deals and reserve your desired travel dates, you should start doing research well in advance. Lodging facilities will often handle their own Space-A program, so you will need to call around and find out who has openings and when the best times are to travel. If you plan to stay on a military-owned recreational facility, you should try to make your reservations months ahead of time. Some even book rooms a year in advance. In other situations, last-minute travel plans are possible because of the fluid occupancy rates of these hotels. The best approach is to call around and start asking questions at your potential destination.

Book Your Space-A Lodging Today

If you are ready to jump in and start planning your next family vacation, it's easy to get started. Once you have some potential travel dates in mind, start checking with military branch websites to find available destinations. You can also search for available lodging at the location you want to visit at www.dodlodging.net.

Web Resources
Air Force Inn – af.dodlodging.net
Army Travel – www.armymwr.com
Marine Lodging – www.usmc-mccs.org
Navy Lodge – www.navy-lodge.com

Military Space-A Lodging Information – www.military.com/benefits/space-available-lodging

Free or Discounted Camping

When you are planning a budget-friendly getaway or just looking for some outdoors adventure, campgrounds can be a great solution. There are military campgrounds all over the United States that offer free or discounted stays to active and retired military members and their families. Some private campgrounds also offer military discounts. Your options are almost unlimited! Each campground has its own policy about who can stay and what fees may apply. Do your research, and you will find new, exciting places to camp all across the country.

What to Expect at Military Campgrounds

On installations around the nation, campgrounds range from simple RV parking spots to new, fancy resorts. Many of the nicer military campgrounds offer full hookups, cable, Wi-Fi, and onsite amenities such as showers, recreation facilities, and even kitchens. Plus as an added bonus, most of these military campgrounds are on active bases, so you have close access to other military-base amenities such as swimming pools, computer labs, and tight security.

Best of all, most military campgrounds welcome children. Many even offer playgrounds and activities for the kids. The littlest campers in your crowd will also enjoy exploring the open areas of the base and playing on the baseball fields, tennis courts, and picnic areas.

Who Can Stay at Military Campgrounds?

Each campground has a policy about who is eligible to stay and how much it costs. Some require reservations while others operate on a first-come, first-serve basis. For example, campgrounds operated by the US Army will waive day-use fees for active service members and their dependents with proper ID or the America the Beautiful Military Pass.

Camping fees are generally waived for active military or DoD members and dependents on mid- or post-deployment leaves. You can find out more specific information on campsite availability and fees by visiting Recreation.gov or calling 877-444-6777.

What Are the Best Military Campgrounds?

There are hundreds of military campgrounds to explore, and you could easily trek your way across the country and stay at a different campground in every state along the way. However, there are a handful that are personal favorites and come highly recommended by other military campers. Check out these top five military campgrounds and start planning your next camping adventure.

1. Admiral Baker RV Park

Located in gorgeous San Diego, California, the Admiral Baker RV Park is a perfect destination. It's close to some of the country's best golf courses, and there are unlimited sightseeing opportunities. You can visit the nearby San Diego Zoo or take the kids to Sea World for the day. There is plenty to do on the campsite as well with playground equipment, a pool, picnic areas, volleyball and basketball courts, baseball fields, tennis courts, and horseshoe pits. The US Navy operates this campground, but it is also open to the public. Military members qualify for discounted rates.

get.dodlodging.net/propertys/Admiral-Baker-RV-Park--Picnic-Area

2. Agave Gulch FamCamp

Nestled in the heart of Tucson, Arizona, the Agave Gulch FamCamp is a top-rated military campground open year-round. It books up fast in the winter months, and it's easy to see why! This campground received the Campers' Choice Award for "Overall Best Military Campground" every year from 2007 to 2011. You will find 198 full hookup sites, an outdoor pool, Wi-Fi, a large commissary with movie rental service, two fitness centers, and even a dog park. http://www.dmforcesupport.com/FamCamp/famcamp.html

3. Krueger Recreation Area

Spread across 160 wide-open acres, you will find Krueger Recreation Area on the McConnell Air Force Base in Kansas. This campground is fully stocked with family-friendly activities: a driving range, disc golf course, archery, remote-control-car course, ATV tracks, paintball, fishing, and picnic areas. Best of all, unlimited rental equipment is available to make your stay really incredible. www.refuelmcconnell.com/recreation/outdoor-recreation/krueger-recreation-area/

4. Cliffside RV Park
Washington's Cliffside RV Park is hands down one of the most beautiful military campgrounds in the United States. Situated on the shoreline overlooking the Strait of Juan de Fuca, Vancouver Island, and the San Juan Islands, it boasts 57 RV campsites plus several tent sites. You can even book a furnished yurt facing the shore. All the RV sites have water and electrical hookups, plus there are restrooms and showers easily accessible from anywhere on the campground. You will enjoy days of exploring the private military beaches

where you will find seashells, pretty rocks, and sea-worn driftwood.

www.militarycampgrounds.us/washington/clifside-rv-park

5. Seabreeze RV Resort

If you are dreaming of a summer beach adventure, look no further than Seabreeze RV Resort in Seal Beach, California. Located inside the Naval Weapons Station, it's private and secure. There are 85 concrete RV pads and hookups for water, electric, sewer, and even satellite television. The Seabreeze RV Resort offers bathrooms, showers, laundry facilities, walking trails, and even an area to wash your RV or car. You'll enjoy barbecue grills, volleyball courts, horseshoe pits, and even a playground. Plus, you will find the 27-hole championship Navy Golf Course only five miles away. Just a half hour from Disneyland and minutes to area beaches and shopping malls,

the Seabreeze RV Resort is the way to go if you are looking for a camping adventure the whole family can enjoy.
militarycampgrounds.us/california/seabreeze-at-seal-beach

Web Resources

Camping and Day-Use Reservation Policies – www.recreation.gov
Unofficial US Military Campgrounds Directory – www.militarycampgrounds.us

Free Access to National Parks

One of the BEST military travel discounts and benefit out there is the US National Park's Service Free Annual Pass to Active Duty Military members. The National Park Service, as many military families are already aware, is host and protector to some of the most inspiring and beautiful landmarks in the U.S. including The Grand Canyon, the Statue of Liberty, Jamestown and many additional natural and man-made sights. United States national parks span 84 million acres of fields, forests, and beaches. If you are looking for the perfect vacation on a budget, national parks can be a great solution! If you are a military family, you can enjoy all the beauty of

America's best national parks for free thanks to a new benefit called the Annual Pass.

What Is an Annual Pass?

An annual pass is your golden ticket—free admission to national parks and government-owned land across the United States. While the pass won't get you free campsites or boat launches, it will get you into the park. Then you can ask if other military discounts are available on rentals.

Who Qualifies?

This pass is available to active duty military personnel. To get your pass, just visit any park or federal recreation site and show your CAC or DD Form 1173. The free annual pass eligibility includes current Army, Navy, Air Force, Marines, the Coast Guard, the U.S. Reserves and the National Guard members.

Traveling with Friends or Family?

Of course many active-duty military members have family and/or friends who are not active-duty military. Does this mean that they have to pay for their own annual passes to U.S. National Parks and other national sites? The answer for the most part is no. With the active-duty military free annual pass all those traveling in a non-commercial vehicle can enter any U.S. national park free or the active-military duty member can be accompanied by three adults who will also enter for free. The free annual pass for active-military duty members truly offers outstanding benefits that allow friends and family to come along for the ride

What about Veterans and Seniors?

While the annual pass isn't available for veterans, you might quality for another discount pass. If you are 62 years or older, you can get a Senior Pass from any federal recreation site. If you have a permanent disability, you can qualify for a lifetime disability pass that grants you access to all federal recreation sites.

Why Visit National Parks?

There are dozens of reasons that national parks make the perfect destination for your next vacation. First, you can observe some incredible scenery, ranging from majestic mountains to breathtaking canyons to gorgeous coastlines. National parks also provide an opportunity to explore what makes America such a great country. You can see incredible nature sanctuaries and observe endangered animals in their natural environments. You can explore historic sites and see remnants of the Civil War and the earliest pioneer civilizations. There is something for everyone, no matter what your interests might be.

Fun for All Ages

National parks provide a great family-friendly vacation because there are activities for the whole family to enjoy. Explore miles and miles of hiking trails, camp overnight under a canopy of stars, or practice some survival skills as you pitch a tent off the beaten path. There are plenty of opportunities for fishing, canoeing, or kayaking.

The athletes in your family will love adventures in places such as Yosemite National Park where rock climbing abounds. Visit Essex National Heritage Area in Massachusetts to try out your skiing abilities. You can even visit the Virgin Islands National Park for the ultimate snorkeling adventure.

The Best National Parks

If you are ready to grab your military annual pass and start exploring the nation's best parks, here is a list of destinations you don't want to miss.

1. Yosemite National Park

In the heart of California's Sierra Nevada Mountains, Yosemite National Park features breathtaking scenery. You can explore dramatic cliffs, gorgeous waterfalls, and wide-open meadows full of blooming wildflowers. The wildlife will keep you guessing with common sightings of roaming deer. However, you might even spot a bear or coyote lingering in the forests, so keep your eyes open at all times!

2. Acadia National Park

A contrast to western expansive national parks, Acadia offers unparalleled views of the Atlantic coastline. It is also home to the tallest mountain on the East Coast. Check out the park's program schedule for a chance to participate in its many unique beach activities.

3. Big Bend National Park

While it might not get as much notoriety as some of the larger parks, Big Bend National Park is one of the best gems in Texas. This park is scarcely crowded, so you have miles and miles of wide-open space to explore with rivers, canyons, and the gorgeous Chisos Mountains perched in the distance.

4. Sequoia National Park

If you want a trip that you will remember for a lifetime, use your military access pass to visit Sequoia National Park. With huge, ancient redwoods standing guard over the park, you will discover a rich history and enjoy a vacation you will never forget.

5. Great Smoky Mountains National Park
Set in the Southern Appalachia mountains, the park offers breathtaking views of forestry and diverse plant culture. Waterfalls, horseback riding, fishing, and more are available at the park. If you have ever wanted to experience the Appalachian Trail you can do a short day hike in the park.

6. Glacier National Park
Deep in the heart of Montana is majestic Glacier National Park, which offers 700 miles of solitude and hiking trails. Spend the days fishing in Lake McDonald or hiking through the pristine forests. The park also features a rich history lesson with historic chalets and Native American artifacts.

7. Yellowstone National Park

As one of the nation's most popular national parks, Yellowstone has a long-standing reputation as a must-see destination. You can enjoy the sights and sounds of Yellowstone all year long, but spring is by far the best time to visit. You can explore miles of hiking trails, camp near the waterfalls, or take a guided tour to learn all about the park's rich heritage.

As you can see, national parks make an incredible choice for your next vacation destination. Take advantage of your active military status and get an access pass so that you can enjoy free admission to national parks around the country.

For the Fishermen of the World
In addition to all of the 397 national parks to which active-duty military members can gain free entrance the pass also grants access to sites managed by the U.S. Fish & Wildlife Service, the Bureau of Land Management, the

Bureau of Reclamation, and the U.S. Forest Service. That means fishing in the Gallatin National Forest in Montana and outings to some of the greatest foliage found in the U.S.

Web Resources
National Park Service - http://www.nps.gov/index.htm

Recreation.Gov Annual Pass – Military
www.recreation.gov/marketing.do?goto=/ATBPass/military_member.html

Information, Tickets, and Tours

As you plan your next vacation, don't forget to take advantage of military discounts available at bases near your destination. By simply showing your military ID, you could get major discounts on sporting events, amusement parks, world-class museums, or watersports! Almost all military bases have an office called Information, Tickets, and Tours (ITT) under their Morale Welfare and Recreation (MWR) program, which we'll touch on later. Just stop by the ITT office and score great discounts on your tickets for area attractions.

When you buy your tickets through the ITT office, you won't just get big discounts. You could also avoid paying facility fees and taxes.

Plus, the service is fast, and the expert staff know exactly what you are eligible for from the moment you walk in! The ITT offices also provide information packs and brochures about nearby attractions. In many ways, the ITT staff act as your personal travel agents, suggesting the best places to visit and offering you the best prices on tickets and tours.

Most ITT base offices have websites you can search for before visiting an area. For example, if you're visiting San Diego, simply Google "San Diego ITT office." You will be directed to the local ITT website, which will list ticket prices and other discounts to preview before you go!

Who Is Eligible?

Access to these discounts is really quite simple. You just need a valid military ID card or some kind of proof of your association with the DoD. The discounts are open to active duty, Reserve members, National Guard, and even retired military along with their family members. As with any discount, it's always good practice to call ahead to confirm the discount applies to you.

Save Money on Tickets near Home

The ITT office isn't important only for vacationers. It can also benefit you when you are stationed in a new area and want to check out some of the local attractions. Maybe you've just been stationed at Camp Pendleton and you want a family-friendly activity for the weekend. The ITT office can hook you up with discounted tickets to go whale watching. If you are at Fort Belvoir, the ITT team will plan a fun day trip to New York City for your whole family to enjoy. From minor league baseball tickets to discounted admission to local movie theaters, the ITT office can connect you to all the best local activities.

Cut Costs on Your Next Vacation

If you are planning a trip out of town to go camping, check out a beach resort, or even visit Disney, the ITT office can help you plan your whole adventure from start to finish. For instance, if you want to take the kids to California, the Offutt Air Force Base ITT office can connect you with discounted tickets for Disneyland and Lego Land. If you plan to visit Washington, DC, you can get discounted tickets to the International Spy Museum or Capitol Segway Tours. What about a family camping trip to Missouri? The ITT office has discounts waiting for the Dixie Stampede dinner show or the popular Titanic Museum.

What Are the Best Discounted Destinations?

The ITT office can unlock a lot of savings for you and your family. Bring along your military ID, and they can help make the trip of a lifetime. Check out some of the incredible possibilities!

Amusement Parks – Get discounted admission to the country's best amusement parks. The ITT office can provide you with discounts for Busch Gardens, Kings Dominion, Hershey Park, and Water Country USA, plus much more!

Sporting Events – Do you love watching your favorite teams play? The ITT office can help you get discounts on tickets to NBA and NFL games. These organizations are proud to honor military members with discounts, and that is all arranged through ITT.

Disney – Whether you are planning a Disney trip to Orlando or California, the ITT staff can arrange for discounted park admission and even low-priced lodging within the parks.

Concerts – If you live for the next great concert, talk to the ITT office about discounted tickets to upcoming concerts. They offer regular discounts for events at the Hampton Coliseum, Ferguson Center, Constant Center, Sandler Center, and Kennedy Center.

Circus – Every kid should go to the circus at least once! It's an unforgettable experience that you can make possible for your family with ITT's discounts on the Ringling Bros. and Barnum & Bailey Circus.

Movie Theaters – Date night just got cheaper thanks to the ITT office. They can provide you with discounted admission to AMC and Regal Movie theaters across the country!

As you can see, the possibilities are practically endless. You can save money on hundreds of fun attractions and tours. Visit your ITT office today and ask about the best discounts in your area!

Web Resources

Marine Corp ITT – www.usmc-mccs.org/ITT/
Navy ITT – www.navymwr.org/itt/
General ITT Info – www.militaryonesource.mil/mwr?content_id=272003

Morale, Welfare, and Recreation Programs

The military's Morale, Welfare, and Recreation program makes life a little sweeter for troops during their downtime. They offer pools, organized sporting events, bowling, and fitness centers on military bases around the country. Plus, they have offices at most installations, so you can rent recreational items such as fishing tackle, beach chairs, coolers, and more. Check out some of the incredible options that the MWR offers.

Sports

Have you always wanted to try your hand at archery? Do you want to get in some range shooting in your spare time? The MWR office can provide you with rental equipment and discounted access to facilities where you can make those sporting dreams a reality. At many military installations, the MWR provides sporting activities such as skeet, archery, target practice, and even hunting and fishing. Some installations have Rod and Gun Clubs where outdoor sports enthusiasts can get together for a day of fishing in the stocked ponds or streams. Do you need to rent archery equipment or fishing tackle? No worries, the MWR has everything you need on hand.

Pets

The MWR benefits extend far beyond sporting equipment. They also make special accommodations for your pets and your love of animals. Some installations offer safe places to board horses. You can even find some bases with riding rings, and they might offer riding lessons to military kids. In most cases, these activities are far cheaper than what you would find outside the military base.

Most installations also offer dog parks so that your furry friends are free to run and play. Most of the time, the MWR lays some basic ground rules for pets, such as up-to-date vaccines, curfews, and mandatory supervision, so check with the office to find out the rules before you take your pet out to play.

If you are traveling on short-term orders, the MWR might also offer you low-cost boarding services for your pets. They generally have daily or weekly fees, depending on your needs. This can be a lifesaver if you get emergency orders and have to leave right away. You can feel confident that your pets are safe and well cared for while you are out on orders.

Events

The Morale, Welfare, and Recreation programs also assist when you need help planning a big event. Whether you are planning a wedding, a backyard barbecue, or a birthday party, the MWR staff can help you line up low-cost options for facilities, catering, and even entertainment.

Outdoors

If you like to spend your free time outdoors, the MWR has plenty of options to keep you busy. From scuba diving equipment to surfboards or snow skis, you can rent all the outdoor equipment you need by visiting the MWR. While the available equipment will vary depending on your location, you can get the scoop on the most popular outdoor activities by talking to the friendly staff at the MWR.

How to Contact the MWR

Each branch of the US military has its own separate Morale, Welfare, and Recreation program. Check out the links below to get started; then you can ask your branch about available activities or amenities.

Web Resources

Army MWR – www.armymwr.com
Navy MWR – www.navymwr.org
Coast Guard MWR – www.uscg.mil/mwr/
Marines – www.usmc-mccs.org
Air Force – Search Air Force MWR by base

Military Campgrounds – RV Parks App

With your free active-duty military national parks pass you may be planning on visiting some beautiful sites and creative works in the U.S. (the Grand Canyon or the Statue of Liberty) or maybe you are planning on taking a camping trip. Either way, you can find U.S. Military Campgrounds and RV Parks (Fam Camps) available to you for FREE with the "Military Campgrounds – RV Parks" app. This app allows you to find the camps, stay for free, access campground map filters, filter campgrounds by amenities, and look up data by region (state, city,etc). In addition, the NOAA weather reports are based on the camps' GPS locations and not the cities or airports near the locations which is another benefit.

Military Discount Soldier App

The Military Discount Soldier app is one of the most popular apps for military personnel. After all, everybody loves free or discounted items.

The Military Discount Soldier app allows you to scan through discounts that are available near you based on your GPS location. Once you've found a discount that works for you the Military Discount Soldier app enables GPS to lead you to that discount. If you know of a discount that is not listed the app allows you to share and receive credit from other Veterans and military personnel. I've added quite a few myself that I discovered.

In addition to the benefits already described, the Military Discount Soldier app is useful for active duty soldiers, reservists, Veterans, retired military, National Guard members, the Coast Guard, etc. Don't miss out on this app.

Military Cost Cutters App

The Military Cost Cutters app provides similar information to the Military Discount Soldier app except that the benefits are focused on Veterans. Veterans of any branch of the military can take advantage of Veteran benefits and discounts anywhere they are available. Searches can be made by city, state or by zip code and GPS location search is available anytime you need to hop in a car, cab or plane to go. Additional benefits are included such as QR-code scanning functionality, discount rating, business reviews, and the ability to upload discounts from a mobile device.

Another benefit of this app is that you don't have to be in the military to use it. For example, you may have a family member or friend who is a Veteran and you can download discounts and share them with him or her. It's a great deal and fun to use when you care about a Veteran.

MiliSOURCE Veterans Benefits

It's amazing how many veterans remain unaware of the benefits that are available to them. Maybe it's because there are so many benefits available and they are difficult to track. Veterans could enjoy these benefits if they were aware of them and could access them in a short amount of time.

The MiliSOURCE Veterans Benefits app allows users to create a personal profile and based on that profile, the app in return provides recommendations for activities and products available to veterans at free or discounted rates. An entire database of 900 federal and state Veteran Service Organization benefits are also available for viewing or via specified searches. Discounts are obtained via deals and/or coupons from leading merchants and any information from the Veteran's Benefit Guides ("VA's Benefits Guides") can also be accessed.

In addition, a one-tap access call can be made to the closest benefits agency where benefits experts can explain all available options. The MiliSOURCE app will also keep Veterans up-to-date via email, social networks and more. Downloading this app is a must for Veterans!

Military Benefits and Military Apps = Savings

We live in a day when accessing military benefits is available with the use of technologies that are easy to utilize. Take the time to play around with these recommendations.

Web Resources

Google Play –

https://play.google.com/store?hl=en

Top West Coast Military Only Beaches

Looking for Military Only beaches on the west coast but want to avoid the crowds? Military only beaches are less populated and offer all the beach amenities that you need for a great vacation. Below I cover just some of the locations to get an exclusive vacation at a rate you can't beat (usually free).

Military Only Beaches on the West Coast: California

California is home to 32 military bases many of which are on the coast or nearby.

Camp Pendleton's Military Only Beach

Forty miles north of San Diego you will find Camp Pendleton. It's likely you've heard of Camp Pendleton because it's the Marine Corps' biggest base on the West Coast. It's property includes 17 miles of beachfront which for active-duty Marine Corps personnel is the perfect place to take a much needed break. Camp Pendleton offers discount lodging for military personnel.

As a side note, public beaches near Camp Pendleton include San Onofre State Beach and the Del Mar Jetties known for its more intense beach break. These beaches are great places if you are lodging on base but just want to get away from the military atmosphere for a bit.

Ventura Country: Naval Base

Also located in California, Ventura County's Naval Base provides military only beachfront. The base is between: Point Mugu and Port

Hueneme. Point Mugu is military only and provides great waves for surfing. During certain times of the year the waves aren't as good as others. If you're a surfer, do your research before. Point Mugu also is the location of a military-run Beach Motel & RV Park. The Motel and Park is available for longer stays and surfboard rentals as well as gear rentals.

Santa Barbara: Vandenberg Air Force Base

Vandenberg Air Force Base in Santa Barbara offers the best surfing on military only property in California. Vandenberg has RVs and tents sites six miles from the beach. This makes it a convenient location for a beach escape.

Military Only Beaches Beyond the West Coast: Hawaii

If you venture far west you could end up at another West Coast in Hawaii. Hawaii is known for its ALOHA spirit, delicious pineapples/mangos, unique dancing and entertainment (e,g, Hula and fire throwing) and many more "Hawaiianisms." Hawaii is also the home of several military only beaches that can't be missed.

Hawaii Marine Corps Base

Located on the east side of Oahu is the Marine Corps Base. There are two military only beaches here. Both beaches offer prime surfing opportunities for lovers of "the swell." The breaks can be challenging (a consistent 6-10 foot break is the norm) but it's an opportunity that surfers can't miss. The other beach location, Officers Breach, enjoys similar surfing opportunities. There is also a nearby park where you can relax, eat, and then walk down to the beach for more surf and sun.

Joint Base Pearl Harbor-Hickam

Also located on Oahu, is the Joint Base Pearl Harbor-Hickam beach. Like the other Hawaiian and Californian beaches in this article it offers surfing. This beach also rents surfboards and provides private surf lessons if you are willing to pay a bit extra. Nearby you'll notice planes touching down and taking off from the base's airstrip which is built, at least in part, into the ocean.

Coast Guard Air Station Barbers Point

White Plains Beach reserved for coast guard members is yet another popular surfing spot. Board rentals are available as are surfing lessons (both private and group classes). Beach cottages can be rented for longer stays.

Barking Sands Pacific Missile Range Facility

On the island of Kauai, the Barking Sands' Majors Bay beach located on offers surfing, shower facilities, parking and cottage rentals for longer vacation times. The beach also is home to Shenanigans, the base's bar and grill, which will keep the hunger at bay with tasty eats. This beach location also rents surfboard, boogie boards, kayaks, camping equipment and other popular beach items.

Disney: Big Discounts from Mickey

Disney is the happiest place on Earth, and no one deserves happiness more than the hardworking troops of the United States military. That is why Disney makes it a priority to offer exclusive discounts to active and retired military members and their families. With theme parks, cruises, and other incredible attractions, there is plenty to see and do on your next big Disney adventure. Check out the best military discounts for Disney at all their most popular destinations.

Disneyland Discounts

Located in beautiful Anaheim, California, Disneyland is the perfect place to spend a few days or even a few weeks with your family. Disneyland offers a lot of great discounts for military personnel, but the best deal is the three-day "Park Hopper" pass. By visiting your local ITT office, you can get up to six of the passes for $132. That's a 42 percent discount off the normal price! The only rule is that one of the six passes has to be used by the military member or his/her spouse. This deal is eligible for active and retired military, Guard, and Reservists. Bring your military ID along so that the discount can be verified at the park's entrance gates. For more information on military discounts for Disneyland, visit https://disneyland.disney.go.com/offers-discounts/military-park-tickets/.

Walt Disney World Discounts

If you are looking for an East Coast Disney adventure, opt for Walt Disney World in Orlando, Florida. By showing your active or retired military ID, your family can get up to six park passes. They currently offer four-day "Park Hopper" passes for $177, a huge savings off the normal price. Even better, you can save more money by staying at Disney resort hotels. Walt Disney World offers military families up to 40 percent off the cost of accommodations at select resorts. For more details, visit https://disneyworld.disney.go.com/special-offers/military-4-day-tickets/.

Hilton Orlando Lake Buena Vista

For the ultimate Disney experience, you want to stay in the Downtown Disney resort area. A perfect choice is the Hilton Orlando Lake Buena Vista Hotel, which offers a military discount. It's a short walk away from Disney shops, theme parks, and the exciting Cirque du Soleil. When you stay in the Downtown resorts, you get complimentary transportation to all the Disney theme parks plus access during after-hours exclusive park times. As a military member, you can save up to 40 percent on select Downtown Disney resorts!

Military Discounts on Disney Restaurants and Shops

As a military family, you can also enjoy major discounts on food and shopping during your Disney vacation. In Downtown Disney, there are numerous places to eat and shop, but make sure you try Raglan Road, an Irish pub that provides a 20 percent discount to military members. Another great choice is the Ghirardelli Soda Fountain and Ice Cream Shop. They offer military members a 20 percent discount, and you can fill up on ice cream, chocolate, and incredible fountain creations. If you're in the mood for some music, visit the House of Blues Orlando. They have a famous Gospel Brunch on Sundays that is a lot of fun for the whole family. Best of all, you can get a

25 percent military discount on your meal and an extra 15 percent off all merchandise.

Military Resorts in Orlando

For the best deal on your Disney vacation, consider staying at the Shades of Green Resort in Orlando. This is a luxurious family resort owned by the Armed Forces. They offer 586 large guest rooms, complete with private patios, tropical gardens, and balconies from where you can watch the sun rise. The resort offers restaurants, golf, and plenty of fun for the kids—all at a steep discount if you are a member of the military.

Plus, when you stay at Shades of Green Resort, you get to enjoy the Disney theme parks longer. Each day, the parks open an hour early and stay open up to three hours late just for the guests at Shades of Green and select other resorts. This is a great time to visit the park because lines are shorter and you have more space to enjoy the rides.

Plan Your Trip to Disney Today!

To start planning your family's magical Disney vacation, you can browse military discounts online or visit your installation's ITT office. Check out the following resources to see current military-friendly ticket and lodging specials:

Web Resources

Disneyland Military Discount – https://disneyland.disney.go.com/offers-discounts/military-park-tickets/
Disney World Military Discount – disneyworld.disney.go.com/special-offers/military-4-day-tickets/
Shades of Green – www.shadesofgreen.org/

Hawaiian Holiday: Dream of an Oahu Vacation

Hawaii is one of the most military-friendly states in the country, and it just so happens to be one of the most exciting vacation destinations as well! Whether you are an active or retired member of the US military, you can get incredible discounts on Hawaiian travel. From accommodations to equipment rental to discounted tickets and tours, there is no end to the benefits you can enjoy when you visit Hawaii with a military ID! Let's check out some of the best options for military travel to the Aloha state.

The #1 Resource for Hawaii Military Discounts

Hawaii's Family Morale, Welfare, and Recreation Center can basically turn your military ID into a discount ticket for activities all over the state. Located in Oahu, the FMWR offers major discounts on tours, attractions, and even vacation packages. This should be the first place you check for discounted tickets when you arrive in Hawaii. They will guide you to some incredible budget-friendly fun!

Military Hotels

Hawaii has a steady stream of military visitors, so they have established several budget-friendly accommodations for the troops and their families. One of the top-ranked options is the Hale Koa Hotel in Honolulu. Military members can stay here at only a fraction of the price of other Hawaii hotels. Discounts are based on your military ranking, and if you are at a lower pay scale, you will pay less per night.

The best time to stay at the Hale Koa Hotel is during the off-season from September to December. During these months, the hotel is less crowded, and you can often get even steeper discounts on lodging.

The Hale Koa Hotel offers upscale guestrooms with either a king, two queens, or two twin beds. Each room includes a coffee maker, refreshment cabinet, iron and ironing board, hair dryer, and high-speed Internet. There are also two restaurants onsite, with two dinner shows, a comedy club, and a Sunday brunch that you just can't afford to miss. You will also find multiple snack bars if you need to grab a quick meal or drink. There is even a health club and spa!

Military Camps

If you prefer a more rugged experience, opt for Kilauea Military Camp inside Hawaii

Volcanoes National Park on the Big Island. This has been a popular military recreation area since 1916, and it offers comfortable amenities without the foot traffic of tourists. You can stay in cottages ranging from one to three bedrooms. Each cottage comes fully stocked with a hair dryer, iron and ironing board, microwave, mini-fridge, and beach umbrellas. Some of the larger cottages have full kitchens and whirlpool bathtubs.

For the cheapest accommodations, you can rent a bed in a shared dorm room on the military base. This offers a chance to meet some new friends and swap military stories. Plus, you'll get all the nice amenities available to the cottage tenants: a community room, video games, sports courts, laundry facilities, Wi-Fi, and even a bowling alley. Plus there are two restaurants, a coffee house, and a lounge onsite.

Non-Military Accommodations

If your family would rather stay in a non-military hotel, you can still enjoy discounts as part of the US military. Eligibility will vary depending on the hotel, so you should call around and ask what special promotions are available and mention that you are a member of the military. The Hawaii FMWR will be a good resource to help you find the best deal on hotel accommodations.

Discounted Hawaii Cruises

Did you know that your military ID could even get you substantial discounts on cruises? Most of the major cruise lines offer trips to Hawaii, and if you are an active or retired member of the US military, you could go for a reduced rate. If you are traveling with a large group of friends or family, check for Carnival's "Friends and Family" promotions. These promotions are available only a few times per year, but if you can get the timing right, you can get all the reserved cabins at the same rate as your military discount! This could add up to major savings, especially if you are traveling as a large group.

As you can see, Hawaii is a perfect destination for members of the US military. With a heavy military presence already in place, there are endless opportunities to enjoy the beaches, hike through the jungles, or climb the mountains—all at discounted prices. To learn more about military discounts for Hawaiian travel, check out the resources below.

Web Resources

Hawaii Military Guide – www.hawaiimilitaryguide.com

Official Hawaii Military Guide – www.himilitary.com

US Army MWR Hawaii – www.himwr.com

Tokyo Travel: The New Sanno Hotel

The New Sanno Hotel is a high-class, US military hotel located in the heart of Tokyo that offers excellent facilities and accommodations, making it the ideal place to stay for those embarking on military travel, including their dependents and veterans.

Eligibility

The hotel is restricted to the following: visitors who are in active duty, including their dependents; retirees from active duty; disabled veterans; retired reservists and dependents; both widows and widowers; active reservists and members of National Guards; DoD civilians who are currently stationed in Japan and their dependents; personnel of the United States Embassy; and DoD contractors and civilians who may be stationed from outside Japan, and Non-DoD.

You will need to provide a valid form of identification when requested. Failure to supply this could restrict your admittance to the hotel.

As the hotel is for eligible visitors only, it offers a level of exclusivity to guests at very reasonable rates, despite being located in one of the most expensive cities in the world.

Rooms

There are six different types of rooms at this hotel, which include standard twin, single, double, and family rooms; and twin, king, and Japanese suites.

The standard rooms come with the all the usual facilities you would expect from a quality hotel, including bathtub, hair dryer, refrigerators, tea- and coffee-making facilities, television with DVD player, and wireless Internet access.

Suites offer spacious accommodations and include the same facilities as standard rooms with the addition of bathrobes and slippers, a sofa with a coffee table, and free newspapers delivered daily.

The Japanese suite is stunning and offers a Japanese–style bed, with a fantastic view of the Japanese garden.

Leisure Facilities

The New Sanno Hotel has excellent facilities, including a swimming pool and fitness center located on the second floor. The pool is heated, making it suitable all year round and a fantastic place to relax and invigorate.

The Jacuzzi and saunas are ideal for soothing away the stresses after a long day, and children will be delighted with their own swimming pool.

The fitness center has a decent exercise club that includes quality equipment for those wishing to keep fit with a workout; however, there is an age restriction for children under sixteen, who must be accompanied by an adult.

Shopping and Beauty

The New Sanno offers a good range of shopping experiences and even has an excellent beauty salon offering an array of treatments.

Ranging from traditional Japanese items and gifts, to watches and jewelry and perfume, the

Navy Exchange offers a diverse selection of goods for guests at the hotel.

Shutters General Store offers a range of food for adults and babies, ice-cold beers, and a decent selection of wine. It has an excellent florist with some wonderful floral creations, which is perfect for any gift requirements. The Hashimoto gift shop is the perfect place to pick up some souvenirs, offering a good mix of traditional and contemporary choices.

Amit Sanno specializes in pearls and is the place to find that extra special gift.

Restaurants

The New Sanno Hotel provides an astounding mix of delightful food experiences, including traditional Japanese at the Kikuya Restaurant and fine and elegant dining at the Wellington, offering delectable treats and American favorites with an outstanding selection of American wine.

The Emporium is a brilliant family restaurant, making it ideal for those staying with children, and The Sunrise Café serves up some decent coffee, with a mouthwatering selection of foods making it the ideal breakfast stop. Hero's offers delicious, authentic Italian Cuisine in an ambient setting. Fair Winds Cocktail Lounge offers a relaxed setting and is the perfect way to unwind after a long day. It has a very good selection of cocktails and drinks.

The exclusivity of this hotel coupled with its enviable position in downtown Tokyo, with very reasonable room rates, is why it is so attractive and popular for those embarking on military travel and veterans visiting the country.

Web Resources

The New Sanno Hotel – www.thenewsanno.com

Korean Getaway: The Dragon Hill Lodge

Located in bustling Seoul, South Korea, the Dragon Hill Lodge offers a four-star stay to US military personnel and their families. The roots of the lodge date back to the Korean War when its facilities were originally used as a mess hall. With official completion in 1990, the Dragon Hill Lodge became a popular destination for military travel in Seoul. Individual military members and their families often visit the lodge for vacation or use it as a comfortable base for travel to and from South Korea.

Eligibility

The only people entitled to stay at this resort are members of the US military and their families as well as former members and their families. This includes:

– Air Force, Navy, Army, National Guard and Reserve, Coast Guard, members on active duty, and Cadets of Armed Forces Academy

– National Oceanic and Atmospheric Administration Commissioned Corps and Public Health Service

– Retirees from active duty, National Guard, and Reserves

– Honorably discharged veterans with 100 percent service-connected disability

– Involuntarily separated service members under the Transition Assistance Management Program

– Personnel separated under the Voluntary Separation Incentive (VSI) and Special Separation Benefit (SSB) programs for two years after separation

– Former or surviving spouses of military personnel
– Other people and their families who are working under the Department of Defense

Resort Highlights

The Dragon Hill Lodge offers comfort, convenience, and entertainment that makes it the perfect destination for any veteran vacation or military vacation. Here are just a few of the things you can expect from a visit to Dragon Hill Lodge.

Leisure Facilities

With these top-of-the-line facilities at Dragon Hill Lodge, you can stay fit, active, and relaxed while on your vacation. Available to guests are swimming lessons, personal training, and group training as well.

Restaurants

You won't even need to leave the resort if you don't want to thanks to the fantastic places to eat and wind down. There are buffets, upscale dining, cafés, pastries and candy shops, and even some fast-food restaurants. Bars wielding cocktails and cold beers are also available on the resort.

City Activities

The Dragon Hill Lodge helps its guest to explore the wonderful city of Seoul. Visitors can purchase Discover Seoul tickets right from the front desk and will be able to see the Seoul Tower, Wax Museum, 63 Building, and more. The staff can also sign you up for walking tours so that you can explore the city with a knowledgeable guide. You will also be able to purchase the Seoul City Pass, which includes visits to the major city attractions and a bus tour of the downtown area.

Not only is the lodge beautiful, comfortable, and accommodating, but it is also a meeting place for fellow veterans and current military personnel. Guests will be surrounded by their fellow countrymen and can together enjoy a vacation that is well deserved. You will always have someone to chat with over dinner, coffee, exercise class, or a tour of some of Seoul's most famous sights.

Web Resources

The Dragon Hill Lodge – www.dragonhilllodge.com

Alpine Adventure: Edelweiss Lodge and Resort

Edelweiss Lodge and Resort is located in Garmisch Partnenkirchen, one of the most beautiful ski resorts in Germany.

Eligibility

The hotel is restricted to visitors who are on active duty, including their dependents; reservists and National Guardsmen; retired military personnel There are other levels of eligibility, and it is best to visit www.edelweisslodgeandresort.com for the most current eligibility guidelines.

History and Area

Garmisch is situated in southern Germany, in the Bavarian Alps at the foot of Germany's highest mountain, Zugspitze, on its border with Austria. Garmisch and Partnenkirchen were once two cities that existed as separate communities for more than a thousand years, until 1935 when Adolf Hitler administratively merged them to make it easier to host the Winter Olympics in 1936. Garmisch is a cosmopolitan city today, and there is a lot to see on the ski slopes and elsewhere. The season starts in November, and snow lingers until May.

So it was that in this idyllic place, Edelweiss Lodge and Resort opened in 2004. Before that, Edelweiss Lodge and Resort was a complex that belonged to the US Department of Defense (Armed Forces' Recreation Centers).

Around $80 million has been invested in the new complex, and it was also created to be a center for recreation exclusively for active members of the military, retired soldiers, members of the National Guard, veterans and reservists, who can spend a vacation with their families in a really beautiful place. The entire complex was given to the US Army as a legacy after World War II when the Nazis were defeated and this stunning complex was taken over by the US military. It was assigned to the military as an infirmary where soldiers who had just fought in the war were accommodated.

Resort Highlights

Today, the Edelweiss Lodge and Resort is one of the most modern resorts in Garmisch Partnenkirchen. It has more than 250 rooms and apartments, as well as several restaurants, a sauna, a spa center, several swimming pools, and everything else necessary for a luxurious, comfortable holiday. Garmisch Partnenkirchen is one of the few winter resorts connected to the railway line. For those who are lovers of nature and history, Edelweiss Lodge and Resort has the ideal environment.

Accommodations

As for accommodations, Edelweiss Lodge and Resort offers three options: accommodation in hotels, accommodation in cabins, and for all adventurers, accommodation beneath the open sky.

The entire hotel interior is done in a rustic style with high-quality woodwork and decorative details. Standard rooms at the hotel have room for four adults and even a child's cradle. In addition to basic accessories, they are equipped with a desk for those who "have" to work during holidays. In addition to the Standard Room, several types of suites are offered. The

Deluxe Junior Suite, for example, adapts to receive four to six people, and the living room and bedroom are separate. Perhaps the most beautiful apartment in the Edelweiss Lodge and Resort is the Deluxe Loft Suite, which is built on two levels. It can accommodate up to 10 people, and it is great for those who want to spend a comfortable holiday with their family. Besides full equipment, the Deluxe Loft Suite has a balcony with a terrace. Edelweiss Lodge and Resort offers Eco-rooms for those who are dedicated to preserving the planet.

As for accommodation in cabins or alfresco, Edelweiss Lodge and Resort offers the Vacation Village and the Campground. The cabins are of very modern design, and they are ideal for a family of six. These are equipped with all the necessary elements for the perfect holiday under the Alps, which includes even a satellite TV program.

Leisure Facilities

The Wellness Club offers a fitness center, massage therapy, and a pool and hot tub.

Restaurants

The resort's dining options adapt to everyone's taste, offering mostly a combination of European and Anglo-Saxon cuisine with the dominant offering of American and German dishes. There are several locations to eat at the resort. Pullman Place offers excellent steaks and a dining experience. There is also Zuggy's Base Camp, which is more casual as a bar alehouse bistro.

Let your Alpine adventure begin.

Web Resources

Edelweiss Lodge and Resort – www.edelweisslodgeandresort.com

Packing for a Short Getaway: Military Style

Whether traveling for business or pleasure, packing light is key to making travel stress free. For military personnel, it's even more essential to pack light. For military personnel and their families, being on the move is a part of life. Particularly when on leave and at a moment's notice you could have to return to your home station.

Step #1: Look at Your Items and Divide Them into Groups

First things first: You have to decide what items you *need* to take. Lay out these items on a table or on a dresser where you can see everything. Now divide the items into the following groups:

1) Items that you thought you needed but are not essential
2) Heavy items
3) Shoes and socks
4) Shirts, pants and underwear
5) Toiletries
6) Snacks, etc.
7) Uniforms or dress suits
8) Magazines or books

Buy some sturdy rubber bands and some mesh bags (see #6). You will be thankful for these small but helpful items in the long run.

Step #2: Get Real, You're Packing for a *Short* Getaway

Now that you've divided the items into groups get rid of items that you thought you might need, but realized later that you didn't. Yes, you need your deodorant but do you need mosquito repellant in November while you're in Boston? Do you need your largest first-aid kit? Do you need your complete family photo album? The answers to these questions, of course, are no. However, keep in mind that if you do leave something behind and you need it that FedEx can send you most items within 24 hours regardless of your location or my personal favorite: an Amazon Prime purchase can be shipped very quickly to your location.

Step #3: Make the Heavy Items Work For You, Not Against You

No one likes to lug heavy and/or bulky items around. Sore shoulders and tired legs can be the result and that can make your trip miserable. Place heavier items at the bottom of your bag or suitcase. They can act as a form of stability and a platform for the rest of your items. For shoulder bags, placing heavy items at the bottom will place the largest amount of weight closer to your center of gravity (the areas of your body from which you have the most power to lift) which will be helpful when you're walking those long distances at the airport.

Step #4: Shoes and Socks

Shoes can be awkward to pack. They are heavier than most clothing items and are often dirtier as well. Make sure to clean shoes or place them in a plastic bag so they don't get any dust or unwanted fibers on your clothing. At least two pair of shoes are required for most trips (even when you're packing for a short getaway) so wear one pair and wrap the other in a bag. Also, use the inside of your shoes as a storage compartment for your socks. You will be amazed how many pairs of socks can fit inside a pair of shoes. Next, place the shoes and the socks on top of the heavy items.

Step #4: Shirts, Pants and Underwear

Fold pants in half and then lay them over your shoes and socks. If you have multiple pair of pants alternate the direction of folding so they can fit on top of the shoes and socks. Fold shirts in half across their vertical centers (along the button line) and then roll them into small cylinders. Secure these cylinders with rubber bands. Lay these shirt cylinders on top of the pants. Next fold underwear in half as well and roll them into small cylinders. Secure these cylinders with rubber bands as you did with the shirts. Lay the underwear cylinders aside for now as they will be inserted into the bag during step #8.

Step #5: Toiletries

The well-known problem with toiletries is that

they can leak or even explode during hectic situations or extreme temperatures faced during travel. To avoid messes caused by leakage, insert all toiletries into a small plastic bag and release the air from the bag before sealing it. Then, insert the plastic bag into a mesh bag or other small organizational bag that is easily identifiable to you. Place this bag on top of your shirts and pants.

Step #6: Snacks, etc.

For snacks, razors or other small items, categorize these into small groups and place them inside of two or three additional mesh bags. The mesh bags are helpful for quick retrieval of the items that you need fast.

Step #7: Uniforms or Dress Suits

For military professionals, uniforms are often required even when packing for a short getaway. Uniforms can be difficult to pack. Just remember, when you pack a uniform or a suit it will sustain some wrinkles; however, you can keep it clean. To do so, place it in a plastic bag that will protect it from stray dust and fibers. When you arrive at your destination, remove the uniform from its bag and hang it in an available closet. Steaming or ironing are methods are best for quick wrinkle removal.

Step #8: Magazines, Books....and Don't Forget the Underwear!

Place magazines and books around the edges of your clothes and don't forget your underwear. Place the underwear cylinders in the available space that remains in your bag.

Now, take a step back, notice how light you'll be traveling, and have a great trip......military style.

Additional "Packing Light" Resources:

-*"How to Pack an Army Duffle Bag"* - http://traveltips.usatoday.com/pack-army-duffle-bag-62699.html

-*"Military Travelers Packing Tips"* - http://militarytravel.com/INCONUSMilitaryTravel/HowToPackSuitcase.aspx

-*"How to Pack an Army Duffle Bag"* - http://www.ehow.com/how_4895337_pack-army-duffle-bag.html

Best Military Discounts and Resources

There are many organizations out there that specialize in connecting military personnel with these discounts, but here is a look at some of the best options and how they can benefit you.

1. Veterans Advantage - www.veteransadvantage.com
There is no military benefit program with more national recognition than Veterans Advantage. This company has been working to give active and retired military members special discounts and offers since 2001. You can sign up on the Veterans Advantage website to receive your own VetRewards Card. This is a perfect

military ID that protects your privacy and still allows you to capitalize on most military discounts.

Veterans Advantage partners with hundreds of companies, and they personally verify each military member's status before issuing a VetRewards card. This is a huge advantage because you don't have to worry about carrying around your official military ID. It also reduces the chances of identity theft if you accidentally lose your ID and it falls into shady hands.

This company offers discounts to both active duty and retired military, National Guard, and Reserve personnel. They accept all branches and periods of service. They also offer a family-member plan that allows you to share your benefits and discounts with a spouse, child, or other immediate family member.

Some of the discounts include travel discounts from top brands like United Airlines, Lufthansa Airlines, Amtrak, and more; At no extra cost, travel benefit plans like free $50,000 Medical Travel Insurance; At no extra cost, free $5,000 AD&D Insurance Coverage; and At no extra cost, free Global Travel Protection Services.

2. Military.com – www.Military.com
This online hub is the perfect place to score military discounts on everything from Disney resorts to airline tickets. They constantly rotate the newest offers, and you can see eligibility criteria and click through to cash in on the discounts. They feature special military discounts for both active and retired military members. You can even sign up for the Military Discounts newsletter to get regular updates when new incentives become available.

3. Armed Forces Vacation Club –
www.afvclub.com

The Armed Forces Vacation Club is your go-to source for "Space Available" discounts and promotions. They offer a steady flow of discount travel options for military members and Department of Defense personnel. They connect military members and their families with accommodations at over 4,000 locations worldwide. Best of all, you only pay $349 per week!

This means that you can finally take your dream vacation to the sandy beaches of Mexico or to the ancient ruins of Greece. The program is open to active and retired military members, DoD employees, and some civilian employees that work in military support roles.

Most of the locations are available during the off-season or on short notice (usually 10 days or less). Destinations vary according to available spaces in timeshares, but the most common trips are to Mexico, South America, or

Europe. Most of the time, accommodations are in upscale condos with full kitchens, but occasionally AFVC offers stays in resorts.

You can browse available vacation packages online or sign up for Space-Available vacations that give you a full seven nights for just $349. They also offer high-demand trips during peak travel times at discounted rates. Complete your trip with military discounts on car rentals, flights, tickets, and tours. The Armed Forces Vacation Club covers it all!

Take Advantage of Military Discounts Today!

You have dedicated your life to serving your country and now you deserve a little downtime. Use these resources to enjoy a dream vacation, a night out on the town, or a day in your favorite theme park at rock-bottom prices.

Made in the USA
Middletown, DE
05 May 2018